wena
NTSIKI MAZWAI

African Perspectives Publishing
PO Box 95342 | Grant Park 2051 | South Africa
www.africanperspectives.co.za

© Ntsiki Mazwai 2010

ISBN 978-0-981-43981-5

Edited by Robert Greig
Typeset by Gail Day
Cover design by Mycalture
Printed and bound by 4 Colour Print

for bookings...
www.ntsikimazwai.co.za
ntsikimazwai@yahoo.com
management@ntsikimazwai.co.za

Contents

About the author   v

Acknowledgements   vii

Foreword   ix

Wena!   1

Hey black gal!   9

Noord Street taxi rank   13

Kwenzakalani?   15

Some fathers   19

Ghetto princess   21

Famous family   23

After I lost uMama   25

Boy problems   33

For you   35

Thinking of you   39

Uyakhumbula?   41

In my garden   43

Good company   45

If you say that you love me   47

Abuse   51

Age of colour!   55

Hamba!   57

I choose life   61

Love in Soweto   65

Miss What-What   69

My generation   73

One thing remains the same   85

Risen   87

Labels   91

Too much woman   93

About the author

Private school girl from the backstreets

This is no languid butterfly, drifting aimlessly among forced, insipid blooms in an artificial hothouse. Ntsiki Mazwai is a hummingbird. Multi-hued. Bursting with the delight of life. Radiating energy as she drinks deeply of the rich blossoms that sprout wherever they find root, she pours these experiences out in a brilliantly coloured tapestry of poetry, dance and song.

Don't think her exuberance is a sign of superficial infatuation with "art" and "life". Young as she is, Ntsiki is no stranger to deep hurts, confusion, rejection and the cruelty of selfish relationships. The conflict of a culture in evolution, swinging from hip black street rap to western cannons of art and literature is reflected in her poems. This is not a woman who skates on the surface of emotion, but a sensitive being who feels the beauty and power of her art strongly.

Ntsiki is clearly conducting a love affair with words: words as poems, words as song, words as dance and wild combinations of all three. Her first foray into the excitement of her creativity was poetry. Then she realised that she could share those words and thoughts on stage and exposed an electrifying dimension of performance which she took to enthusiastically, finding another aspect of her personality and talents previously unknown. She embodies the issue of identity facing so many South Africans, shifting into "situational identities" rather than stabilising on a fixed, unalterable core identity as we strive to find a suitable merging of sometimes contrasting indigenous and western cultures, values and ideas.

From hugely successful beadwork to written poetry, from poems performed and danced to theatre and music, the constant underlying theme of Ntsiki's work is courage – courage to speak on painful or controversial issues with almost brutal honesty. "The book relates my journeys in a very personal way," she explains. "I want the work to help heal people so that they can tell their stories and then be brave to find their own voice and operate as full human beings, and not as the wounded spirits that fill our world."

Acknowledgements

I give thanks to all the people that contribute to the ever present love and joy that is my life.

My siblings: U my homebase, my crew, my life.

Malaika thank you for believing in my swag!

My beautiful aunts who support me through the learning curves; Enkosi.

To everybody who contributed to this project, thank you, especially Rose Francis, Robert Greig and David Wa Maahlamela.

SIYABANGENA!

Foreword

Poetry comes in different forms, though many academics tend to narrow down their definition of what poetry is; reducing what others may perceive to be poetry, to an 'art' of a lesser, not fully developed form.

However, poet and performance poet (or praise singer), Ntsiki Mazwai, was in this collection brave enough to take a contemporary route free from pretentious metaphors which might at times interfere with a reader's thought and comprehension process. Her themes are the stuff of everyday life; yet she imbues them with a deep sense of verse, while also making it clear that this is neither Wordsworth nor Joyce you are reading.

As she explains in the poem *Famous family*: "*There's no chemistry/ between pen and page/ no make-believe...*" This is actually one of the factors that make her work special. She uses language and figures of speech that do not need the Oxford dictionary (or an intricate understanding of the nuances of traditional verse with its metre structutres and rhythmic cadences), making it easy for the message to be conveyed – which is the principle motive for writing, not so? She is unashamed to open wide the curtains of her heart and share her moments of personal pain, loss and weakness. Poems such as *After I lost uMama*, *Hamba!*, *Abuse*, *Uyakhumbula?* and *Boy problems* explain this better.

One significant poem, *Noord Street taxi rank*, about the young woman who was molested by taxi drivers a few years ago for 'daring' to show up in a mini skirt at the taxi rank in the poem's title, re-sketches this humiliating scene and concludes by exposing the collusion of 'innocent' bystanders, in this heinous act, with "*No one losing their (his/her) place in the queue*".

Ntsiki, a former member of the *Feel-a-Sister* group of poets that included Myesha Jenkins, Napo Mashiane and Lebo Mashile, is one of those poets known for turning tables upside down in the world of performance poetry, yet her expressions, while performing, are never like those of a lioness about to unleash vengeance on another animal that sought to harm her cubs.

I have always observed a perfect symmetry of body language, facial expression and a sweet flow of words during her performances. Interesting thing about her is that as much as she is a Xhosa praise singer in her own right, she can, as in a poem like *Age of colour!*, easily fuse elements of street culture, kwaito and hip-hop in her work.

Ntsiki is also known for her cocktailing of different languages in some of her poetry, which, as this snippet shows, appeals to the youth in the streets: "*Wena!/ O kwankwetla/ Wena! O swere vibe mos./ Wena!/ Bakufuna bonke.*" No wonder DJ Fresh fused his house music with her poem, "*Sana Uwrong-o*", Ntsiki's poetry is music.

Her love of township life also comes through strongly in poems like *Love in Soweto,* which explains the difference between what Soweto means to others and what it means to her. Black consciousness and feminism are also themes that recur in her work, especially in *Hey black gal!, Kwenzakalani?* and *Ghetto princess*. In her autobiographical poem, *My Generation,* Ntsiki shares her experience of varsity life: "*I had learnt the ways of the West/ finally reached a time when/ I wanted to teach the West my ways/ my culture my story/ The dlozi power pulsating through these veins.*"

Two poems which will continue to echo in your head long after you've read them are *I choose life* and *Miss What-What*. Let's conclude with a stanza from *Miss What-What*.

> *So you,*
> *Miss "I went to school with whites all my life" –*
> *Have forgotten the strife*
> *Your ancestors called life*
> *In the struggle to live*
> *The crimes you forgive*
> *Have you forgotten:*
> *The struggle for freedom*
> *The crime, the pain:*
> *Multitudes were murdered*
> *For you to be 'Born Free'.*

All in all, this collection can be summarized with her quote: "I don't write quiet storms". It's only after you've read, that you will understand what she means.

David Wa Maahlamela

Poet

wena

NTSIKI MAZWAI

Wena!

Wena!
Okwang kwetla, boss.
Wena!
O sweri vibe mos.
Wena!
Bakufuna bonke

Too much choice
You're in demand
It's not your fault.
Hamba wena!
Hayi man, wena!
Wena! Wena! Wena!

Bendi kwenye'kasi kuthwa awujoli he
        yake s'thandwa sam
Oyini ntliziyo yam
Kwashukuma umzimba wam
I am strong, black woman – angry
but I have my dignity.
Take this epiphany
you were never worthy
I'll get through gracefully.

O batla eng
fantasy king?
Women just to feel –
nothing but a fling
Well this queen
never wanted your ring.

Wena!
Okwang kwetla, boss!
Wena!
Osweri vibe mos
Wena!
Bakufuna bonke.

Too much choice;
you're in demand.
It's not your fault

Hamba wena
Hayi man wena
Wena! Wena! Wena!

U busy ushaya shaya abantu la ngaphandle.
You forgot
where you came from,
speaking about what you've got.

All I remember:
our love was never a home –
the gifts you never bought,
nights that weren't so hot,
me and empty sheets.

You had your business:
kanti ubusy uyimixa nepleasure.
We were never together:
just a matter of time
before all your lies gathered
but now none of it matters.
What happened happens.

Wena!
Okwang kwetla, boss.
Wena!
Osweri vibe mos
Wena!
Bakufuna bonke
Too much choice;
you're in demand
It's not your fault.
Hamba wena!
Hayi man, wena!
Wena! Wena! Wena!

Have the decency
to operate with honesty.
You could have been more direct,
told me it wasn't for ever.

You lied so blatantly,
slept in so many beds casually

Wena!

Hey black gal!

Hey black gal with issues
Go ahead and junk those tissues.
It's time for liberation:
Sing your song in celebration!

Hey black gal ngehips nempundu hey!
Awusemhle ntaka yamandla
Bendicela ukukubamba isandla
No one works those hips like you.

I know, it's true these hips
are for keeps
to lure the boys.

Hey blak gal ngehips nempundu
Ngamaxesha akho
Stand up and be counted
Hey!

Hey! Black gal with issues
throw away your box of tissues.
It's time for emancipation
Sing your song in celebration!

Hey blue, blue, blue, blue, blak gal hey!
Let it go
Your fear of yellow, red and green.

Sister, where have you been?
The blacker the skin
the more lies they'll create
to try and disfigure
African beauty
Iintsikelelo kuwe
Blu, blue, blak Qhawekazi
Hey!

Hey! Black gal with any issues
Throw away those tissues
It's time for your emancipation
Sing sing sing in celebration!

Noord Street taxi rank

In a denim mini skirt
her long legs carried her
through her city.

Nwabisa, bald headed girl,
in a T-shirt
finding her way home

It was all so sudden
they dragged her skirt up her torso
they grabbed at her panties

She tried to fight
many strangers sweaty
many fingers prising jabbing

It didn't take long
The guards said it was nothing special
People stood, watched

No-one losing their place in the queue

Kwenzakalani?

Mama Afrika, I cry
for all the hunger.
Knowing your abundance,
I bleed.

I need
government to set education free,
to live in a world that's hunger free.

I agree: all man and woman
are equal,
Who says
there is no place for me?
I'll show you the rock in me.
Too many raped souls bleeding,
too many sisters living in abusive silence,
too many infected mothers with no access to
medications,
too many women farmers who can't eat from their own
growing .

Kwenzakalani Ma Afrika
Kwenzakalani?

Mama Afrika ndiyakulilela
No lies,
Being female
eMzantsi kuRough!

Dragged and torn down
the nine-year-old girl
Is seen but not heard
silenced.
Her virginity
no longer her dignity:
misused, abused, used and confused

Who are our revolutionaries?

Kwenzakalani Ma Afrika
Kwenzakalani?

Some fathers

Some fathers of these days
Move in a haze: away.

Your seeds weep.
they seek your love.
Some fathers of these days
break baby hearts:
no baritone lullabyes.

You left my heart
parts you didn't play.
You didn't stay
to hear me say
Tata, I love you.

Some fathers of these days
Left disappointment
in the place of being a parent
left resentment.
They forgot.

Wherever you are, Tata,
whatever you're doing, Ntate
remember me, Baba,

and all fathers of bitter days.

Ghetto princess

I wash dishes,
sleep with a mgusha on my head,
taxi riding … done that!
These are ghetto secrets I hold in my heart.

I burn imphepho to make everything right,
Thokoz' uGogo in the middle of the night.
Big family gatherings, laughter,
massive speakers in the garden:
these are the ghetto moments of my life

At street bashes, djs play me some kwaito.
I love a weekend car wash shisa nyama:
these are the ghetto songs that play in my head

I polish the stoep red
and plan Sunday dress,
go to church and sing black hymns.
We resurrect such powerful spirits –
ghetto melodies touching my core

You will find me in Soweto, Alexandra, Gugulethu,
Khayelitsha, New Brighton, Kwa Mashu,
Emlazi and Emdantsane –
just look for the ghetto princess

Famous family

Way back in 92
I lost my mother
started paying my dues.

I wrote to move.

They think it's blood connections,
a family story:
they think it's shine and glory.

I write to move.

Pain and suffering,
powerful words:
I don't write quiet storms:

I write to move.

There's no chemistry
between pen and page,
No make-believe:

I write to move.

This woman writes, she moves.

After I lost uMama

I don't have time
to tell you
it was a crime.
Now you want peace,
you want me to release

all this anger inside
You accused me
of having an STD!

I cried cried
I cursed you.

Now you
remind me
how you cared
protected me
After I lost uMama.

Don't talk crap,
the cosmic connection –
You gave me the drama
after I lost uMama.

You don't mean to torture
said I was a failure
You say you're ashamed
bringing me into this world!

It leaves me cold
Do you want me older?
"dead?"
You were suppose to parent me
Next
you were gone.

Oh, you never meant to hurt me:
saying I was just a failure
after I lost
uMama.

Quit the crap
the cosmic connection –
You gave me the drama
after I lost uMama.

You should have a say in this conversation –
your words of wisdom cut with precision.
"You're not the first or last to lose a mother"
"Get over it"

Where was my father?

I'm free of all this drama:
I lost uMama.

Quit the crap
the cosmic connection –
You gave me the drama
after I lost uMama.

This verse should curse.
your mission was to shed me
You hate me.
from your bitter vocabulary
I learnt how to swear
And never to care
Though you were slowly killing me.

I knew only terror
with you in my life.
I remember the blue-eye you gave me as a Christmas
present
When he was around
you were fake and phony!

His going let you say
how you hated me
I would fail
I saw all that darkness
stored in your skull.

Quit the crap
the cosmic connection –
You gave me the drama
after I lost uMama.

I'm grown up now
it's every day healing
the aches in my heart
some days wishing
One day to forgive you.

Peace won't come today
Tomorrow is seen through tears
Yesterday just memories.

After I lost uMama.

Boy problems

The problem of being a girl like me
Is the ability
To like more-than-one-boy-at-time.

Ndinithanda nonke!

For you

If you told me art
was the way to your heart:
Canvases of pinks and red
Graffiti tags on the Mandela Bridge
Beaded lamp posts Illuminating the ghetto
Any small gesture

If art would do
I'd be an artist.
For you.

If you told me gentle waters bring you comfort:
On a white sandy beach I'd build our shack
The rains would hear me pray
Everyday
They would hear me say
Let it rain on our crystal domain.

If water would do
I'd be the gentle stream
For you.

Say music was your fetish
I'd resurrect Marvin's soul
Let's get it on
I'd jazz up marimba's passion
With kwai-hop-soul
Make my music your home

If songs would do,
For you
I'd compose
a mass symphony

You call me your queen
I waited for you to let me in.
I bat my eyelids
Crown my lips with a smile
I think: "Damn this man is fine!"
I'm royal jewels,
for you,
I shine.

Thinking of you

My eyes light
Smiles escape
An effect
I can't fein

Every second every hour every day
You're there, inside, watching

Uyakhumbula?

How it all started:
calls: midnight, Thursdays was 'Naked Nites.'
Why hadn't I been at the club?
Where was I?
Hung up the telephone
and drove across town

We played, we flirted
Then – I don't know why – we just fought
I had a stone in my mouth –
Muted love lyrics
Scared of my feelings

My friend tried to get it on with you
I cracked the code you used to tell me
Even in anger, in silence, distance
You must have cared for me

In my garden

I picked up all your cigarette butts,
threw them in the dustbin:

Memories too.

Good company

They arrive
we laugh
Iced drinks
Clouds of smoke
We tell stories
Feel alive
A part of something

Winding down
We say goodbye
Clear the glasses
It's back to me
I think: *they* were good company.

If you say that you love me

These mixed signals
riddles
forgotten cuddles:
you only remember my muddles

They've got me crazy,
wondering if you still love me
too tired to hug
when I go
too quick to call.

I wish you'd just show me
you're mine
And yet I cry
keep checking to the sky
Did I build a lie?
I need a solution
This pain is excruciating.

Am I abusing myself
for the fear of losing
Missing you madly

You have no time to make me happy
Yet you say you are with me
am I just too lazy
to find the love that you give me?

In a lonely taxi:
do you still love me?

If you did then you would show me
surely I shouldn't feel lonely

I'm going
but I keep coming back
So it's true

I must love you:
don't say that you love me
show it.

Abuse

Scared, I stayed with you
A self doubting me
denying, pretending
you weren't hurting me.

Blindly I wanted to be with you
saw only what my eyes would see.
You came and went, came and went
never answered my calls.

I left that space
and half of me
the half of a woman
I didn't want to be

I stayed with me
Not wanting to hurt anymore
cry till I'm sore
wonder where you are at night while I watch the door.
I know: you are behind someone else's.

Tried to silence hurtful truths in my head
tired of the taste of my bitter mouth.
Point broken.

And in hindsight, heavily relieved
I missed out on your diseases, multiple baby mamas

I found in this space,
all of me
more than the woman
I used to be.

Age of colour!

I see their faces
Wearing black, bling and pink goggles
Bright hoodies have become part of my scenery
An exciting backdrop to the intensity
That is my history
Undoubtedly
I am living in the age of colour
They swagger around
Move in gangs
like they have something to believe in
mcees battle just so they can kick a freestyle
dj's play because it's not just about music it's a lifestyle
it's finally happening,
Nothing like my history
Undoubtedly
we're living in the age of colour

They almost seem like they're make believe
Like drawings out of a cartoon strip
With so much character
They know what's hip
Blazing creativity.
Young, Free, Mzansi and Street.
A beautiful product of my history
Undoubtedly,
living in the age of colour

Hamba!

I can't speak for love anymore:
your's was – let's say – disappointing.
My heart breaking,
you forgetting
how you said you'd never leave.

Hamba! Go!
So I can forgive myself,
for thinking there was something.
You were my everything
I was your nothing
I won't blame myself
For your harshness

Who is this?
Who is this woman I have become?
So weak and so afraid.

You make me weak, weak, weak,
so weak, that I weep.
You make me weak, weak, weak
I can't even breathe
You make me weak, weak, weak
– my soul bleeds.

Head bowed
my face in my hands
Gutless, senseless
complex situations
that leave me broken.

Hard to admit choosing my mistakes.
these bruises you see
are soul-deep.
I was battered,
Self esteem in broken pieces: scattered.

I'm past the hatred,
But my mind is still
Pretty much wasted.

Hamba! Go!

I choose life

I wandered aimlessly,
drowsy from the fear of losing.
Abandonment whispering at the bottom of my soul.
but I chose life,
because I knew if I didn't live
at that crucial moment I would die.

I choose life...
Because today's sadness,
must pave the way to
tomorrow's gladness.
I wish that in tomorrow lay all my dreams conceived,
all my hopes conquered,
and all this sadness,
a lesson learnt.

I choose life...
Because my troubles and pain
may open doors to tomorrow's wealth.
I choose the sweetest truths in my life.
I choose giving and sharing,
but sometimes I feel I go without acknowledgment.
My river banks flood with completeness
Every time life smiles at me

Overwhelmed at what I had to experience
Before I made love to love
To know to love
give in to love
let go of love
Even when you still want love around

Touch is a move
I choose life
Because
It's a blessing to be Alive.

Love in Soweto

Some say it's the ghetto
Breeding murderers,
rapists and thieves.
Funerals every week

Not for me
I found
A lover, a care,
Tender walks under dusky skies
Hand in hand,
Soweto lovers chat
At a chesa nyama sessions
We established the initial connection
Some kind of salvation
for my almost lost
faith

Some say it's the ghetto
World famous poverty,
Broad day light robbery
Hungry kids
Scattered like scavenging animals

Not for me

the sun shines on my path
Dusty street lovers
telling stories through our bodies
Sunday afternoon music singing our love art
Street playing children composing our song
In mkhukhu melodies
We kiss
4 room harmonies
we caress
Corner big house
happiness
Tenderness
Loveliness

Some say it's a ghetto
But I
I found love in Soweto.

Miss What-What

Miss "I can't say your name properly"
Have got an identity crisis clearly
You're made up so sadly
To put it quite plainly
Our black names are sighs of divinity

So you,
Miss "I went to school with whites all my life" –
Have forgotten the strife
Your ancestors called life
In the struggle to live
The crimes you forgive
Have you forgotten:
The struggle for freedom
The crimes, the pain:
Multitudes were murdered
For you to be 'Born Free!'

Well,
Miss "now just because I have fake hair doesn't mean
I'm not African" –
Your warped version of foreign beauty
Has got you confused 'shawty'
Kuse Azania la
isikhathi sokungazazi siphelile

It's clear Miss Plastic
I am black, Brown, mahogany proud
Known for kinky hair
A tiny waist
and voluptuous hips.
And sometimes it's a shame
When I see you disowning your own
heritage

Well,
Miss. "I've never been to Soweto"
Don't front like you don't have a multi-class family
Always concerned about being part of the elite society
How do you expect to find harmony
if you can't decide your loyalty?

Hardly Miss Azania
it's a mission
And not a competition.
However,
I expect complete recognition
Of this systemized delusion
That has created SO MUCH confusion
In the final redemption
Of Afrika's Creation

My generation

I was born and raised koKasi.
Kasi life, Kasi parents, magwinya, fish and chips
just like any kid in the township.
English was TV
attempted islungu twangs
I speaked de langwage .

Seven years old at white schools
Igama lami.
mutated
from Nontsikelelo to Nonsiki to Nsik, to Seeki.

How do I even spell that?

I had to fit in.

My own people wondered
at this name with no meaning:
pronunciation tested friendship.
Black in my world
someone had to teach me what Nontsikelelo
meant: "The mother of blessings"

I remained
an ignorant black, a stupid black,
who-did-not-speak-English black.

you could even tell apart blacks who spoke English
from the masses of blacks
They dressed fine.
I did not want to be seen
as a shady black

At primary school
I was busy being a better black
I did not play diketo
Just teddy bears and Barbie dolls
fronted like I didn't know
masihlalisane 4-4.

I fitted in.

Embarrassed to be seen in a Golf
My little brother hides under the bonnet
When I drop him at school
He hopes to elude
eyes of rich kids who are cool

Glass was between black and white worlds.
We didn't discuss politics or race.
In primary school we pretended
At high school we separated

Grade 3 class:
Whose fault was the mess?
Who stole the land?
Who got the goodies?
Sang the national anthem discordantly

Who has a silver spoon in their mouth?
How can I love you?

Lost we tried to find each other, our generation.

Reached high school, hiding behind makeup to mask
my identity.
Asked: "So: what's your father the boss of?"

When puberty hit
Shipped to Queenstown, Ekomani.
Yah neh, my father's bright idea.
From Jozi to reality.
City girl tangled in grass

Black was the majority.
To raw Xhosa girls.
I spoke funny
In no time at all
they straightened me out
My mother tongue is explicit
with not much room for diplomacy
In the land of the Xhosanostra
there was no place for an English Xhosa girl
to hide.

It's not cool
I had been brainwashed.
It's not cool to not know your own language.
My language is who I am.
Language is who you are.
What is the price of fitting in?

I sit at a dinner table
I am mgqusho
I am papa

Sent back to a private girls' high school
I learnt my place
How it always changed.

I watched the elite surrounding me
money ate like acid
Changed faces.

What was the struggle?
Black economic empowerment dreams
broke families
Wealth divided
Those you love from those you are loyal to
Generation X with
Heartbreaking family histories
survival stories form every face.
Such great expectations.

Yet freedom blessings fall like rain.

My university daze:

My mother's family was poor.
My father's family was rich among poor.
Too old for pocket money
Too young for a job
But I knew I had a purpose

I had leant the ways of the West
finally reached a time when
I wanted to teach the West my ways
my culture my story
The dlozi power pulsating through these veins.
A time to celebrate my history
Who I am

If it feels this good to shine my light, then I wish you the
same.

I meet the world in Mzantsi streets.
I meet the world in myself.
I make the future
I hear your culture
Now listen to mine

I am not lost
My world is not lost
Never.
My life is a flowing river

One thing remains the same

Before:

Dusty feet ground thumping
Big body grace
Hand clapped rhythm
Strong voice harmony
I love to see African women
Dance

After:

Stilettos elegant at the club
Sexy bodies winding
Hips swaying wildly
Music igniting passion
I love to see African women
Dance

Risen

I refuse to surrender to fear any longer
I open my closets
So set my skeletons free.
This voice I have been given

Ntsiki speaks!

My mama named me "Blessing"
so hiding from my light
would be blasphemy
Anointed my name with divinity
This voice I have been given

Nontsikelelo has risen!

This poem, like a prayer, was written
To be said again and again and again
As I am rising
to deafen the sounds of fears,
that bang in my head.
It's time to claim
This voice I have been given

Ntsiki speaks!

No more punishment.
I take responsibility
Recognise my vulnerability
Use the gift I was born with
These words that flow freely
The voice that is me.
This voice I have been given

Nontsikelelo has risen!

Labels

Strong: for my experiences
Humble: for my connectedness
Bitchy: for not accepting less
Harsh: for my direct truthfulness

Sweet: for my giving ways
Funny: for the stories I enact
Aloof: for this they call me names
Arrogant: when I don't want to interact

A goddess: for my powerful words
A queen: with nations to reign

Too much woman

I believed in you
when you weren't worth believing in.
Stood tall
by your spineless changes of character.
I was insane
to search for sense in your craziness
a foundation
in shifting winds.

Our memories are forgettable,
you were never there
to create them.
I'm not crying I want you back
My tears are not for wasting.
I have left our empty room.

Lose my number,
erase all memory:
you never knew me.
You tarnish my reputation.
I am not weak

I was too much a woman for you
We know it.

Other titles from African Perspectives Publishing

- *Azanian Love Song* by Don Mattera
  ISBN: 9780620394864
- *Memory is the Weapon* by Don Mattera
  ISBN: 9780620394871
- *The Silent Scream* by Sulette Gardiner
  ISBN: 9780620412452
- *Dancing Sermons* by Bishop Trevor Mwamba
  ISBN: 9780951447024
- *Nostalgic Waves from Soweto: Poetic Memories
  of the June 16th Uprising* by Solhra
  ISBN: 9780981439808
- *The Politics of South African Football*
  by Oshebeng Alpheus Koonyaditse
  ISBN: 9780981439822

African Perspectives Publishing also distributes:

- *Flying Above the Sky* by Lebo Mashile
  ISBN: 9780620412414
- *Brazil: A Century of World Cup Football* by Anthony
  Akpan Ikpong
  ISBN: 9780980076837
- *The Empowered Native* by Letepe Maisela
  ISBN: 9780620335614
- *Politics is the Greatest Game* by Pat Stevens
  ISBN: 9781857565669
- *The Centre is Black* by MGN Kahende
  ISBN:9781857564389
- *Tehaka's Journey* by Murray McMillan
  ISBN: 9781857566079